MW00626441

With gratitude to the students of

The Falls Church and

Forest Hill Church

Copyright © 2018 Nick Dusenbury.

All rights reserved. This book or any portion thereof may not be reproduced or used in any manner whatsoever without the express written permission of the author except for the use of brief quotations in a book review.

Front cover image by Corinne Johnson.
Book design by Corinne Johnson.

Printed by DiggyPOD, Inc., in the United States of America.

First printing, 2018.

www.generous-city.org

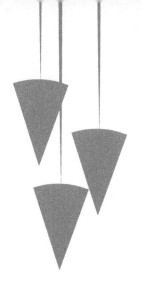

CONTENTS

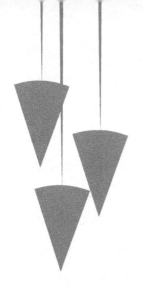

INTRODUCTION

This is a big moment. Huge. You won't have many of these. A chance to change your life and maybe the world along with it. High school is done and now you're likely either in college, in the world of employment, seeking employment, or some combination of the three. I used to believe that as soon as I was done with high school, or college, or the job with the crazy hours, that life would finally slow down. What I came to realize, as many of you have already realized, is that life doesn't stop. Once you finally see that big milestone in the rear-view mirror, you shift your attention to find that there's another milestone in front of you.

A lot of life changes as we go, but one of the things that stays pretty constant is our concern about money. Money can reach deep into every corner of our lives. It can affect our self-image, what we worry and dream about, as well as our families and relationships. And, like life, money doesn't stop either. It's always swirling around us, whether we are dealing with a lot or a little. Multiple times a day we are thinking about it, talking about it, or watching it come and go.

So what makes this moment – this season – such a big deal? Because this is the calm before the financial storm in your life. I'm not saying it's a storm in a bad way, I'm only saying that there's going to be a lot more activity, bigger numbers, and bigger stakes than you're used to with your money. In other words, when it comes to money, it's about to get real.

Big decisions are coming up – decisions about where to live, what kind of place to live in, what kind of car to drive, what kind of social life you want to have. Some of these happen without putting any thought into them, and some happen more intentionally. But there's an even bigger decision looming that makes the rest of those questions look small, because it has the ability to change the course of your life, the lives of others, and maybe even the course of history.

Ready?

>>>

Here's the biggest decision – how *generous* do you want to be?

Not the first question you thought you'd decide on, right? Here's the deal - money can change your day, but it can also change someone else's life. It can even change their eternity, if you think about it. Being generous with our money is usually somewhere on our list, but it usually comes after a lot of other things. The more I speak with people in their 40's, 50's, and 60's, the more I hear from them that they wish they could be making more of a difference with the money they've been given. They're having a hard time being generous now because they never asked that one big question at the beginning. They asked it 20 years later, after all their money was wrapped up in debt and other things and now they don't have room, or the willpower, to change things up.

This isn't a book about living in a box and eating grass so that you can give away everything you have, but it is a book about the idea that the money we're given (whether as salary, or gifts, or anything else) comes from our Creator for us to use however we see fit. Because our Creator also has asked us to help bring heaven to Earth, we want to think carefully about how we use what's been given to us (here's a hint…it's not all for us.) It's not natural for us to think about what we have in this way, mostly because we've spent a lot of our time taking in lies from multiple sources about how debt is great, and that it's all really "our" money and "our" possessions.

I don't know where this book finds you. I do know that this is a great time in your life to think about the kinds of things you really want to do with money. You're going to be entrusted with way more of it than you're used to from here on out. I hope being generous is one of the things you want to do with that money, but that's really between you and God. And no matter where you are, it's helpful to plot out a course for where you're going.

Not having a plan for your money is like not having a schedule for your day.

Sure, it's fun for a while, and then you realize you're missing out while great opportunities pass you by. And if making a plan that will help you look back on your life and feel great about how you handled the money that came your way is an attractive goal to you, then this book is for you.

Goals

Years ago, I had to take an exam so I could be licensed as an accountant. The exam was two days (yes, days) long and covered everything I had learned in college and more. This is not an exam you wait to study for the night before. The only way I could make sure I prepared well and covered all 230,000 topics (I embellish, but only a little) was to break down the topics and plan to study particular topics on particular days. The plans I made became my goals each day, week, and month. The goals I set helped me stay focused and eventually helped me reach the big goal of passing the exam. I'm sure caffeine played a role somewhere in there, too.

4

You've likely had plenty of "goals" in life before, even if you've never played soccer or hockey. Goals help give us direction in our busy, day-to-day lives. With them in mind, goals help us make good decisions when faced with tough choices. If I had a goal to lose 10 pounds, and it mattered to me, I would make better decisions in the smaller moments that make up my day. If I have set that goal beforehand and keep it in mind as I go through all those daily decisions, I'm more likely to reach my goal.

Money goals work the same way, and if you've never made a goal related to your money, don't worry, it's really easy. For now, think about what's most on your mind that's related to money. Right now. Go ahead, I'll wait here. Got it? Great. Now think about something that you want to do about whatever you thought about. If you thought about something to save for, or getting a credit card paid off, think about how you'd do it; if you thought about wanting to give more of your money away or of making a difference in the world, think about how you'd do that. When you think about the how, be specific and realistic.

Being specific is important because we want something that we can turn into an action step, something that brings our goal into our everyday world, so we can see progress. Being realistic is important because we want to be fair to ourselves given our current situation. Sure, it would be great to solve the clean water crisis in the world or pay off all our debt with an unexpected bonus, or winning a reality television show, but neither of those quite meet the definition of realistic. Let's stick with what we know for sure about our financial world (and yes, you can still hope to win American Ninja Warrior, just don't count on it.)

Here are some examples of financial goals to keep you thinking:
>>> You've been lax on paying off your credit card in full each month, and now you owe $400 that you don't currently have.

>>> Specific and realistic goal: To have your credit card paid off in full four months from now.

>>> You heard about a crisis in another country and learned that you can sponsor a child in that country to help them get food, water, schooling, shelter, and counseling. You've got the money to sponsor one child at $35/month.

>>> Specific and realistic goal: A year from now, you want to triple that and be sponsoring three children.

>>> You've heard from your older sister, who just graduated, that she has monthly $300 student loan payments she now has to start making. She tells you to avoid student loan debt as much as possible. You decide she's right. While it's not realistic for you to land a job while you're in school that pays for all of your tuition, you can certainly put a dent in it.

>>>   Specific and realistic goal: To contribute $3,000/year to your tuition so you don't have to take out loans for it.

>>> You've convinced yourself that you're a poor, starving college student who doesn't have money to give right now. But, you've also started to become more concerned about those in need around you and you're starting to believe that maybe it's not all about you after all. You want to get started on being more generous.

>>>   Specific and realistic goal: You're going to start giving 10% of your money away, and everything else you need to live on will have to find a way to fit into that other 90%.

Obviously, setting the goal requires that you'll still need to make it happen. Maybe that means you'll have to spend less on something. Maybe it means you'll find another way to make some money, like taking on a part-time job (or two) during the summer. We'll get more specific about the "how-to's" a little later on.

>>>

There's almost always a way to see our goal happen - the question is how important it is to us.

If a goal is important to us, we'll make time (and money) for it.

Keep your goals in mind, as well as how good it will feel to reach them. Doing that will help you make better choices as the days go by. For now, stick with 2-3 goals at most. Trying to reach more than 3 goals at once can get frustratingly slow. Cross some of these first goals off your list, and you can move on to the next ones.

The List

At the end of some chapters, we'll provide a list with a few re-minders. Remember that this whole thing is a process. As much as we like checking things off of our list, this is more of a list of reminders than it is a list of things that need to be done today. The lists will take some patience but I hope they provide direction and a spirit of accomplishment when you get to cross them off your list. I would encourage you to have one or two that you're always working on so you can see the progress that you're making. If there are any below that you've already done, congratulations! Your reward is checking off that little line.

___ Make a list of all of your financial goals, including things like paying off debt, giving, and items or experiences you'd like to save for:

_____

_____

_____

_____

_____

_____

_____

_____

___ Pick 2-3 that you'd like to focus on right now and put your goals in priority order:

_____

_____

_____

These are very real decisions that can set your life on a completely different trajectory than if you had never thought about them. These decisions can make the difference between regret or celebration in your life and the lives of others. I know it feels like a lot, but it will be well worth it. This book is here to help. I want you to get to a place where you can meet your financial goals, while at the same time seeing how the resources you've been given can impact the world around you in positively amazing ways. My prayer is that the decisions you make here and now will echo in wonderful ways for all eternity.

Ready?
Let's go.

CHAPTERONE

THE FIVE LIES//GIVING

Life's most persistent
and urgent question is,
'What are you doing for others?'
-Martin Luther King, Jr.

At no time did it cross my mind that diving headfirst into the Atlantic Ocean with my glasses on wasn't the best idea, but there I was. And there went my glasses. My only hope for clear vision getting washed away by the current. I'm reasonably certain they became the very expensive home for some lucky shortsighted hermit crab or other ocean dweller. I was a college student home on winter break, volunteering with high schoolers at our church student retreat. During Saturday afternoon, there was a five hour block labeled "free time." The concept of free time inspired lots of creative ideas about what you could do in and around a hotel, at the beach, in the middle of winter. So, of course, running into the ice cold ocean when it was 48 degrees outside somehow seemed like the highest and best use of our time. Not that it was my idea, of course. But I figured if these students eight years younger than me could do it, so could I. Not a great moment in resisting peer pressure, especially since I was the "leader."

I spent the rest of the week bumping into walls and calling everyone by the wrong name. "Yo!" became my go-to greeting, with the person's name left out. I also spent the week worrying about how to pay for another pair of glasses. My parents had long ago stopped paying for replacement glasses for me. I know that sounds cruel, but after 320 replacement pairs in my lifetime they had to draw the line. As we got on the bus to go home, one of the other leaders stepped onto our bus, hat in hand. But he wasn't asking for anything. Instead, he presented me with a small miracle – a hat filled with cash! This was money that had been collected, student by student, dollar by dollar, specifically to buy me a new pair of glasses!

Three hundred and twelve of the crinkliest, dirtiest, dollar bills (some folded into airplanes, of course) were crammed into a dirty baseball cap. That didn't matter to me, because they all represented an overwhelming answer to a prayer generated by hundreds of people in a very tangible way! A group of teenagers had again impacted my life in a meaningful way.

Before they handed over their crinkled money, each of those teenagers had a moment. A moment where something helped them decide this dollar bill was better spent on someone else than on themselves. That something was generosity. My attention was immediately drawn to the impact that the generosity of others could have on a life. I had been told about generosity over and over again. I had even dabbled in it here and there, but it wasn't until I received it in such an incredible way that I understood. My perspective had shifted completely. Is this what generosity felt like to those who receive it? I didn't want it to stop with me. I wanted it to keep going. Truthfully, I don't think any of us want to get to the end of our lives and look back and see we weren't as generous, giving, or life-changing as we could have been.

But that's the struggle. The opposite of generosity, focusing on "me", is crazy popular these days. It's very easy to believe. Almost all we see and hear around us tells us to keep what we have to ourselves. After all, we earned it, and we might need it someday for something we want. It's not a new struggle. In fact, it's one of the oldest challenges out there. Even people back in Biblical times were wrestling with the same thing. I believe what's written to them (and also to us) can begin the process of changing our perspective and helping us remember what truly matters.

Paul, one of the founders of the Christian church two thousand years ago, talks through this generosity struggle in a great passage in I Timothy 6, in verses 17-19. Paul uses this part of his letter to a young pastor, Timothy, to show him and us that when we understand it correctly, generosity brings a new and radical perspective on what matters.

The perspective it brings changes what matters because it gets right to the heart of who we were created to be. God values relationships above everything else – our relationships with Him and with each other.

> >>>
>
> When we give, it feels good because it's loving others by giving of ourselves — exactly what God did for us.

This new perspective is hard to hear because we're constantly being bombarded with lies that point us in the other direction. These lies sounds good, and they're everywhere. They come in forms of advertising, peer pressure, and what we observe about how the world works. And believe me, if you haven't heard them yet, you soon will. We even might have gotten some of them from our own families. Let's break down a few of them:

Lie #1 — You Can't Escape Your Past

Whether you realize it or not, a large part of how you view money was shaped by how your family approached money as you grew up. As you read through this book, it will help for you to think about how money was treated when you were younger.

Did you feel rich or poor growing up? How did your family handle money? How did your family express generosity? How
much did they talk about money or generosity?

Your answers will likely be all over the place. However, the real
point is to wake up to the fact that money (and generosity) are
now yours to make decisions about. For sure, God's word can
help you make those decisions. Wise people in your life can
help guide you.

>>>

But what you actually do with the money you
are earning or receiving is now your call —
no one else's.

God has officially entrusted you with those decisions!

This is a valuable thing to keep in mind as you make decisions
about the kinds of things you want to do and change with your
money. Maybe you feel like your family lived most of your life
trying to get out of debt, or never had anything saved up for
emergencies, or wasn't as generous as you'd like to be. Whatever the case, now is the time to think about how you'll approach those same decisions differently. If you don't stop and
think about it now, you'll likely repeat the past.

Lie #2 — Generosity Is Important, But Later

Very few people intend to end up bankrupt, unable to be generous people, or living beyond their means. It happens through a series of decisions (choices they make) and circumstances (choices made for them) that lead them to those places. Making a decision now to handle your money both generously and wisely is a very important step. Trying to make this decision later is infinitely more difficult. Sure, later you'll make more money. Later, things might not be as stressful (although you might be surprised). The "later" approach, however, has been shown to lead people to never be as generous as they want, and also to miss out on opportunities around them right now. It's a lot easier to move toward generosity now, before life gets more complicated. You get to choose now whether to make it part of your life or not.

Some people feel like they don't have much to give, but God doesn't care how many dollars we're talking about here. That's not how He looks at money. What matters is how generous you're being with what He's given you. That is your responsibility. It's about faithfulness, not financial statements. Pay no attention to those in the public eye giving away millions or billions. That's to be commended, but you are connected to the God who multiplied five loaves of bread and two fish and fed over 15,000 people.

> Even the small amount you can give now, doing it with a cheerful and generous heart, will have deep and eternal impact.

So, where are you? Are you starting your first job or career, or waiting to? Are you just doing some work on the side? If you don't have many expenses, it's even better. Wherever you are as you read this, your best time to decide how generous you want to be is this moment. Right now. Choose a number, maybe a percentage of what you receive each month. Give that amount, and let the other expenses line up after your generosity. Let them fill up the rest of your spending after you've set aside your giving.

See what we did there? We flipped the lie on its head. Yay, us.

So give that amount, and as you start making more money, you've already made room to be generous. If you've already made big commitments about where you live and how much rent you pay, and you can only give some, then give that some. Then, set some goals around being generous and start thinking about ways to be able to reach your generosity goals in the future. We'll get to how to set and meet those goals as we go through the book.

The most important thing is to get started. Then you can increase and adjust the amounts you're giving as you fall more and more in love with generosity. A popular speaker and teacher, Andy Stanley, is quoted as saying, "Generosity won't happen unless you make it a priority." Putting a roof over our heads, food in our stomachs, these things will happen.

But we have to be intentional about it if we want see the life change that only comes through generosity.

Taking some time once or twice a year to think about your generosity and financial goals will do you (and those in need) an immense amount of good. Decisions you make right now will have dramatic effects on both your future and the futures of those you are able to impact. I'm excited for you as you think through these decisions!

Lie #3 — "Mine"

My favorite word when I was two years old was "mine." I said it about things that I had in my hands, and I usually said it about everything anyone else had in their hands, too. This was particularly true if what they had in their hands was edible. It's still something I have to wrestle with regularly. You too, huh? The "mine" myth runs deep and wide, friend. That would make sense, given that it's pretty much how we arrive in the world. We are led to believe and even outright told (by some) that everything that comes your way, whether you worked for it or not, is yours and no one else's. Forever. Period. It's hard to recover from that.

Most of our parents helped keep our stuff in check so we didn't go overboard. But now that you're more on your own, you've got to find your own way to make sure you don't "mine" yourself into a place you don't want to be – a life that looks selfish, uncaring, and prideful. What will you believe? Will you believe it's really all yours? Or could you believe that it's all God's, and He's entrusting it to you? This is not a small decision you're about to make. It shapes how we approach much of our lives, so choose carefully.

Lie #4 – Safety First, and Second, and Third, and…

A few years ago, I came across a popular speaker who was (rightly) encouraging people to start saving for retirement while they were young. His listeners were told that if they start saving $1,000/month in their early 20's and were wise with their investing, they could have $15 million when they retire. Then they could live off of the $40,000/month they would get off of the interest from all that money and life would be good. While that sounds like a great plan, my question is, "then what?" What in the world are you really going to do with $40,000 a month? I know that sounds amazing when you hear it, but really, just stop. Think about it. There's a line where we simply have too much.

The problem is, so many of us cross this "too much" line without even noticing it. I know you're laughing right now because you feel so very far away from "too much". Maybe you've heard the wise saying that if you wanted to cook a frog (yes, I know, but bear with me), you can't throw them into pot that already has boiling water in it. They would hop right out. Instead, you put them in the pot and then slowly raise the temperature. They will cook right up (yum, right?) – the gradual change isn't enough for them to feel the danger and change their situation.

Our turn toward greed and selfishness is usually just like this, slow and subtle.

In the Bible, in Luke 12, Jesus tells the story of a rich man who already has more than enough to take care of himself. On top of all that, he has an amazing year on his farm (back then your farm was your money). So after sitting and asking himself what he should do with his extra, he comes up with the answer. We want the answer for him to be, give some away! But he comes to a different conclusion – keep it all! He built more barns to keep all he had received for himself, just in case. He figures, a little bit more is the only thing that can really make him feel like he's set and prepared for anything the future can bring. The story doesn't end well for the rich man. He gets to the end of his life (sooner than he anticipated), and dosen't have a good answer for how he had used everything he had been entrusted with. He kept way more than he needed, just in case. It's likely that this mindset was developed slowly with hundreds of small decisions about only trusting himself in life.

Talk to anybody about how much money they would need to feel good about their financial situation, and they usually will tell you, "a little bit more". You'd probably say it about your situation right now. Most of us don't want to be greedy, but we do desire to be safe. And even though safe sounds like a reasonable goal, listen carefully to this next sentence:

>>>

We can never get to the place where money can make us safe.

We hear of people who are millionaires, and we think that if we were in their shoes we wouldn't have a care in the world. But if you talk to those millionaires, they will tell you all the things they worry about. They worry about their possessions, the stock market going down, taxes going up...the list goes on. They might even share with you that they envy the billionaires because they would like to be like them and have nothing to worry about. See the pattern? They have tons more money than we do, but they still worry about a lot of the same things! We can never have enough to feel "safe". Another lie turned on its head.

The secret here, as you might have guessed, is that we're supposed to rely on God for things like safety and contentedness. We should not rely on money to do those things for God. Relying on money for our safety and satisfaction is just an empty promise. Sadly, most people spend their whole lives trying to get things with money that only God can provide. Alternatively, we can believe and trust that He has our backs. God teaches us that yes, some of our money is to be used to take care of our needs and the needs of our family, but not all of it. But as we give out of what God has provided us, our generosity helps those in need rely on God as he moves our hearts to help them. It's a really amazing cycle. But when we keep it all for ourselves, never believing enough is enough, we break up how the cycle is supposed to work.

Proverbs 30 pleads to God, "Give me neither poverty or riches, but only my daily bread. Otherwise, I may have too much and disown you and say, 'who is the Lord?' Or I may become poor and steal, and so dishonor the name of my God". Stealing is obviously wrong, but so is depending on things so much that you forget about God. This proverb focuses on the line in the middle, namely, depending upon God for our daily needs. Most of us are in far more danger of replacing God with our money than we are of needing to steal to feed our families, so we need to pay close attention to when enough is enough.

Lie #5 — You'll Miss It When It's Gone

Ever heard someone regret something from their past? Sure, we all have. I regret the time I started a prank war in my freshman dorm in college (which somehow escalated to a day where everything I owned, including electronics, was drenched in Gatorade. It's a long story.) I also regret some of the opportunities I missed to be courageous about expressing my faith in the same dorm.

People usually share these regrets as a reminder to themselves of the lesson they've learned from that experience. Their hope is also that we (the people listening) will use that knowledge to avoid similar choices in the future. We pay attention because we don't want the baggage or regret that comes with those decisions. To paraphrase, "ain't nobody got time for that."

In the past decade or so of talking with people about their money, I have heard multiple people share much regret over past financial decisions they've made. Maybe it was about buying a house before they were ready to take one on, or getting that latest gadget that wasn't worth it or broke after a month. Some are regretful about not having done more good with their money in the past, or spending everything they have on themselves.

But just as helpful to us as paying attention to what people regret is paying attention to what they don't regret. As I've mentioned before, never in all of my time working with people and their finances have I ever heard anyone regret money or resources they gave to those who were in need. Whoa, wait a minute. An investment with no regrets, that gives back things more important than any stock or company we could ever invest in? Yes. Generosity actually has a triple impact when it's given from a generous and cheerful heart to those who are in need.

Read on, readers.

CHAPTER TWO

TRIPLE IMPACT//GIVING

[You] are to do good, to be rich in good works,
to be generous and ready to share,
thus storing up treasure for [your]selves
as a good foundation in the future,
so that [you] may
take hold of that which is truly life.
I Timothy 6:18-19

There are a lot of things you can do with your money. But really, there's only three – spend, save, and give. This book will cover all of them. Hopefully you've read enough about the lies and the truth in the last chapter to understand that generosity – the giving part – isn't just something else that we do with our money, it's actually a world changer. Here's three big reasons why:

First, the effect of generosity that's easiest to see is its impact on those who receive it. For those who receive the sacrifice of our time and money, their days and maybe even their lives are changed. We see their needs being taken care of, and their hope being restored. I'm not saying it's never OK to spend some of the time, talent, and treasure God has given you on yourself – he gave some of that to us to enjoy. Taking some of our time to renew ourselves and rest like we would on a vacation, or owning things that aren't necessary but are fun to have and contribute to our physical and mental health. For me, a baseball bat is good when I get stressed and need go to the batting cages. These are things that provide needed rest and relaxation. But seeing how our resources can change people's lives is a reminder that...

>>>

...we have the ability to actually join God in what he is doing in the lives of others by being generous.

Maybe you've experienced some of this impact before. Maybe you've heard stories about families that have come to faith because a missionary you or your church helped support was there to talk with them. Maybe it's when you got letters from a sponsored child overseas and you see the impact your small amount is making in their lives. Or even when you shared your knowledge in order to help build a website for a non-profit that can't afford to pay to have one built. It could be when you went to help build or repair a house for a family that needed a second chance. You're spending part of the time, talent, and treasure that God gave us. All the resources God provides for us, they can change our day, but they can also change someone else's life.

Another effect of generosity is that it impacts those who give it (that can be us!)

Being generous draws us closer to the God who created us and is generous toward us.

It's how he created us – the good feeling you get when you give (some have called it "the warm fuzzies") is not an accident or self-generated. It's actually your soul connecting with more of who God made you to be. When we trust in God as our provider enough to give away some of our resources, it feels good because we are getting lined up with who God created us to be from the beginning – generous givers.

This might look different for all of us, and there's not a number or an amount of time that God says is generous enough. Instead, God invites us to have an ongoing conversation with Him about being generous. When it comes to how generous to be, God wants us to wrestle with it. He wants us to talk with him, to keep growing and stretching. If you're comfortable in how you give your resources away now, and you hardly even think about it anymore, I'm going to ask you to have a conversation with God about that – He might be calling you to more. Maybe you leave that conversation and you feel OK with where you are. That's fine. The key is just taking time to talk with the giver of all that you have about how you're using what He's given you. That's always a good use of your time. At the very least, it gives you a chance to be generous, and it gives God an opportunity to grow you. He is after our hearts as givers because that's what He is – the ultimate giver. Not just in the grace and mercy he gives us, but the tools he gives all of us to build His kingdom.

> >>>
>
> It is no wonder that He, the ultimate giver, wants to develop giving in us.

Generosity's effects are not limited to changing us and those who receive it. The third effect of generosity is that the very sight and existence of it impacts those who observe it. You're not the only one who may get to see the end result of what generosity can do in another person's life. There are lots of times where you don't get to see it at all. But you can bet that God sees it and it's also true that others will see that impact as well, and may even come to know better who God is because of it.

And no, we don't want to be the kind of people who make a show of giving. Jesus warned against this repeatedly. Instead, we give and we trust God with the results. The point is believing that the ripple effects from generosity can be immense.

Get Started

If you're having trouble getting out of the starting blocks with generosity, pay attention to the challenge God gives us in the Bible. Check out Psalm 34:8 and Malachi 3:10 – verses about trusting God and testing out this giving thing. God loves it when we give because it expresses our faith in Him as our provider. So give it a shot, even in a small way. See what happens! I think you'll like it. I'm also just crazy enough to believe you'll want to experience more.

Here are some additional tips to help generosity happen with what you've been given to manage:

>>> Instead of worrying about what you don't have, decide that "enough is enough." Draw a line and determine what you have is "enough". Use that to help you redefine what in your life is "extra" that you now can be generous with, whether it's money or possessions. The chapter on spending will help you with this.

>>> Keep the generosity conversation going with God. You can bet that God loves us too much to want to just have one sit-down with us about how generous we want to be in our lives. Let your needs, your wants, and the needs around you help shape your time with God in this area.

>>> Get educated about where you're giving. Most of the time,

your money is best given to organizations which have shown that they take good care of people's donations. Get to know the places you give so you can feel safe entrusting them with what God has entrusted to you.

So yes, we need some of this money stuff to survive and save for the future. But generosity, in a very loose paraphrase of the Bible, is where it's at. Here's a great example that Randy Alcorn gives in his book, *Money Possessions & Eternity*:

"Imagine you're alive at the end of the Civil War. You're living in the South, but you're a Northerner. You plan to move home as soon as the war's over. While in the South you've accumulated lots of Confederate currency. Now, suppose you know for a fact that the North's going to win the war, and the end is imminent. What will you do with your confederate money? If you're smart, there's only one answer. You should immediately cash in your Confederate currency for U.S. currency – the only money that will have value once the war's over. Keep only enough Confederate currency to meet your short-term needs. When we make assumptions about what will last, we can end up empty-handed. When we think with a kingdom mindset, our perspective changes. Within 2 years, the value of a confederate dollar was 6 cents, and it just went down from there. Those who had put their hope in this currency watched it fall apart."[1]

You can probably see the parallel – none of the money and possessions we have on this earth will have any value when we get to our real home in heaven. Yes, we need some money on this earth to meet our needs. But we should also change what we can to the only currency that's worth anything once we leave this earth (Matthew 6:20). I think you'll also find that doing so makes your time here even sweeter, as well.

The List

___ Take a few minutes to think about how your family handled money when you were younger. What do you observe or remember? What do you think you'll do the same? Differently?

___ What are some causes around you that you believe in and would like to be a part of? Make a list here:

_____

_____

_____

_____

_____

___ If you don't currently have a financial goal for generosity, think about creating one. It might be around how much of your income you'd like to start giving away, or an amount of money you want to support an organization you believe in. Make this goal part of your budget going forward. You may have to trim in other areas to make this happen, but I know you'll discover it's worth it!

Generosity Goal: _____

___ Spend some time at the websites of the organizations you give to. Check out websites like charitynavigator.org or ecfa.org to learn more about the organizations you give to and how they use the gifts entrusted to them.

[1] *Randy Alcorn,* **Money, Possessions, and Eternity.** *(Carol Stream: Tyndale, 2003), 100.*

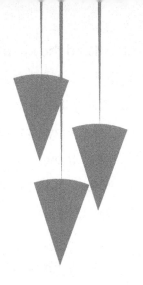

CHAPTER THREE

BEST PLAN EVER//SPENDING

**The prudent sees danger and takes precautions,
but the simple keep going and suffer for it.
Proverbs 22:3, 27:12**

**A budget is telling your money where to go instead of wondering where it went.
Dave Ramsey**

Some of you may have turned here first. It might have looked like the most attractive option in the Table of Contents. Maybe it just sounded fun. And as a fellow spender, I can tell you, it is fun. Spending, like money itself, has the potential to be either good or bad, depending on how we use it. But spending can quickly become not fun when we run out of money to do the things we want to do. It can get extremely not fun when we've run out of money to do the things we need to do.

Some of my friends who had just got married realized they kept running out of money each month, but didn't have a solid reason why. So one month, they wrote down everything they spent money on each day. They figured this was the best way to find the leak. They were right, but they didn't like what they found! They realized that their daily trips to Starbucks were setting them back $500 a month. That's $6,000 a year! That's some leak.

Do you know some people who have to check their bank account before they can do anything that costs money? Or people who will spend and spend as long as they have some money left in their account or limit left on their credit card? Are you one of them? Impulsiveness and money get along great for a while, but their relationship has lots of heartache later on.

> **>>>**
>
> The best way to handle our money is with a plan — normally referred to as a budget.

Since the word "budget" usually brings on sleep, tears, or both, let's think about this like your daily schedule. Many of us have a plan for our day – how we will spend the time that's been given to us. We like/need to know where we have to be that day and how we're going to spend our limited time. We can spend our time well or poorly. We have limits on our time, like sleep. We can choose to ignore these limits at our own cost.

There are lots of similarities here to money – a **budget** is to your **money** as a **schedule** is to your **time** (apologies if I just gave you a bad standardized test word association flashback). How will you spend the time you've been given? How will you spend the money you'll earn or be given?

Budgets Matter

I'm not sure how else to say it. You know the phrase, "money makes the world go round?" Or how about, "money isn't every-thing." While the second is more true than the first, money sure does have a significant say in how your world goes round. Your budget matters not only to you, but also to the rest of the world out there that will be dramatically affected by how you choose to spend, save, or give your money. No pressure, right? Life with a budget will enable you to make plans and follow through with them. Essentially, you're telling your money what you want it to do.

> >>>
>
> Life without a budget means your money con-trols you.

People with budgets have a solid shot at staying out of debt, giving more, and saving more. A life with a balanced budget is a life with less stress, more control, and more generosity. When we let our money make plans for us (life without a budget), we get scared and cling very tightly to money. Over time, living like this can make us more selfish people. But when we make plans for our money (life with a budget), the opposite occurs. We trust more and "selfish" less.

>>>

There's no middle ground here — you have a plan, or you don't.

With four huge areas of your financial life at stake (spending, debt, giving, and saving), you're going to want to get this right. Ready?

Getting Started

Let's keep things simple. Your budget is a plan of what is going to happen with money that comes your way. Many times it's written out on paper, but some people like using apps or websites. Don't get caught up in exactly how you do it, the point is that you do it.

Your budget starts with a simple goal: have no more going out than is coming in. In other words, make sure your expenses aren't more than your income. You've got a balanced budget if, during a month, you can meet all your expenses and commitments. No fair putting expenses on a credit card (unless you can pay it off in the same month). That would be like cheating (see the chapter on debt).

Most people start too quickly. They take a guess at what they spend each month on some pretty hard-to-guess categories. You know the ones – going out to eat, coffee shops, dating, weekend trips, etc. A budget is only as good as the numbers that make it up. It does no good to think you're spending $50/month on gas when in fact you live 25 miles from work and drive a behemoth that gets 8 gallons to the mile. And those $8 lunches add up - having one every workday is about $175/month, or $2,100/year! None of those individual meals feel like $2,100, but when you see them all together, you see the trends. Don't panic, this isn't about saving money by not eating. It's about having a plan so you feel great about whatever you're enjoying with your spending.

Unless the numbers we're trying to estimate only happen once a month (like rent or a car payment), we're almost always wrong about how much we think we spend on the things we do the most. It's like we spring leaks in our spending. If we stop and think about it at the end of each month, those leaks add up to a lot of missing money. I'm not saying we have to stop doing all those things. I am saying that for this budget thing to work, we have to figure out where the leaks are. We have to own them.

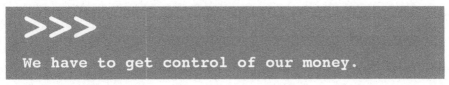

>>>
We have to get control of our money.

Find the leaks
The right place to start is by finding out what we're actually

spending. This will let us see how you're doing now so you can start making a plan, which in turn will help us meet our goals. This means...brace yourself...doing some work. How many of you just winced in pain?

If you're still with me, good – a lot of people put the book down after that last sentence, never letting it see the light of day again. Unfortunately, they miss out. Not you, you're seeing this thing through. Go, you.

The best way to see where your money is going is to track it – find a way to be able to see how each dollar gets spent for a period of time. There are dozens of apps out there that will help you with this. Just search online for "Apps that Track Spending" and you'll be greeted with someone's recent article that points out the best ones. Look for one that will link to your bank accounts and make it easy for you to put your spending in different categories. The easier it is, the more likely you'll make a habit out of using it, and the apps make it pretty easy.

If you want to live a little more "offline", or if you just love pencil and paper, we have just the method for you. Create a chart on a sheet of paper with columns for their various categories of spending and rows for each day of the month. We've got an example for you in the back of this book.

You can also find these kinds of charts online and then print them out. Then place that amazing chart somewhere you spend time every day - a computer desk, bedside table, kitchen, etc. Then take 30 seconds a day (yes, just this is all it takes, sometimes even less) to write down where you spent money that day. And if you can't remember well or don't keep receipts, then carry a small notebook and pencil with you during the day. Then you can transfer that information to your chart of awesomeness at the end of the day.

Some people use a hybrid. They look at their online bank statements containing their debit and credit card spending. Some banks help you put this spending in categories (with a little help from you.) Then they take this information and put it in a chart that makes sense to them.

>>>

When it comes to tracking spending, the right system is one that works for you.

So find one that sounds best to you and give it a whirl. Oh, one other thing. If you ever use cash, make sure you add that to your totals in whatever system you use. We want to make sure we don't have any unrecorded "leaks" going on.

Here are some categories you may want to include in your tracking, whether in an app or otherwise. You can create as many categories as you want, but don't go crazy - the point is to keep it simple and get good information:

- Giving to charity
- Rent/Mortgage/Utilities
- Transportation (gas, parking, car repairs, etc.)
- Insurance
- Groceries
- Eating out/dining/snacks
- Pets
- Personal care (medical, health club, dry cleaning)
- Entertainment/events
- Loans/credit cards
- Savings
- Gifts (birthdays, holidays, etc.)
- Clothing
- Miscellaneous (leave room to write a note next to your "miscellaneous" item so you remember what it was and why it was miscellaneous).

Some of you may be concerned that I've just taken all of your free time away for the rest of your lives. First of all, this won't be something you'll have to do forever. Record all your spending into those categories for a month, and presto - you've got a solid start on a budget. Two months of information is better, and three months is the best. Multiple months helps because it captures things that may not happen every month, like road trips, oil changes, and clothes-buying. For instance, buying clothes for me happens about once every five years. Don't judge. But even after you develop a budget, tracking your spending can be useful if you make a major life change like moving to a new place, starting a new job, getting married, or having kids. A big change in life requires a new plan, and tracking your spending will help you develop the right plan for your new season of life.

If this seems like it takes some self- control and discipline, then you've understood the assignment correctly. Hebrews 12:11 reminds us, "No discipline seems pleasant at the time, but rather painful. Later on, however, it produces a harvest of righteousness for those who have been trained by it."

This is truthfully the hardest part of budgeting, but it's also the foundation of every good budget. So yes, this will take a little time and discipline, but it's a small price to pay to gain control over something that, left alone, will end up controlling you. So don't be afraid of what you might find out, and don't wait for the start of the month - get going!

At this point, it's not necessary to change how you spend your money, we'll do that later (if it's needed). For now, just focus on the tracking. I know it's some work (and some waiting), but remember - this is the whole foundation of your budget. This is the foundation of your financial plan - it's the most important thing you can do right now to get your finances under control.

The List

___ Track your spending for 1-3 months. You can work on other steps while you do this one, but keep this step running in the background.

___ Identify any areas of spending that seem or feel "out of control" to you. Come up with a monthly spending amount that makes sense and find some ways to stick with it each month (track it, use a budgeted amount of cash from an envelope labeled for that category, etc.)

CHAPTERFOUR

GOALS & EMERGENCIES//SPENDING

**A budget is not just a collection of
numbers, but an expression of
our values and aspirations.**
Jacob Lew

When Pokemon Go was released in the summer of 2016, the only stories trending more than how popular the app were stories about people who were ending up in the hospital (or worse) while playing it. The issue? They had their faces buried in their phones and failed to look up on a regular basis to see where they were headed. Sometimes things like cars or cliffs already occupied the space they were moving towards. Yikes.

Your life is busy, and lots of things are happening each day in your finances. Money comes in, money goes out. We can choose to ignore looking up and just make sure we have enough money for today, or we can choose to look where we're going. Sure, it feels fun to live in the now, and I'm not suggesting that you don't ever do that. I am suggesting you don't get surprised by things like cliffs, speeding cars, and things that can upend the budget you're working hard to create.

So, after we total things up, we're going to add two more things to our budget. One helps us from getting stuck, and one keeps us moving forward. Let's dive in.

The Envelope, Please...

Once you have a picture of where your money is going, it's much easier to answer the question, "how much do I usually spend on _____ per month?" Before, we were taking guesses. Now we're focused. But we're not just playing trivia here. Having the answer to that question for all the ways we use our money will help us see the bigger picture. The next step is to get everything on one page or one screen so we can see what's coming in and what's going out at the same time.

Take the information from your tracking (good job, by the way! You did it!) and use it to create a list of your average spending in all of those categories for each of the months you tracked. If you spent $100 in gas one month, $150 in another, and $140 in another, then your new gas budget number is $130 (the average of the three months). Do this for all your spending categories.

Now make sure you add in once-a-month expenses like rent, or insurance to give you a full picture of your normal monthly expenses. Add your income to the top or bottom of the list, and congratulations, you have the first draft of your basic budget! Well played. Take a breath. A pat on the back for you. But as I mentioned, we're not quite done yet. There are other things happening in our financial lives that we have to budget for, too, if we want this to work.

Surprises That Aren't

Some people love surprises, some people don't. Budgets, however, hate surprises. When an unexpected cost comes along, (a car repair, a busted refrigerator, etc.), it blows your budget to smithereens. We give up. But fear not, it doesn't have to be this way. We can stick to our budget better when we can anticipate some of those things that we know will happen to us. We do this by saving up for those things we know will happen eventually.

You may have experienced some of these things in one of your months when you tracked your spending. There are also other things that only come up once a year or even worse, once every couple of years.

After a few years of renting, I decided to take the plunge and actually purchase a house. A few roommates helped make the mortgage payments happen and I had a budget for a few bumps and repairs here and there. One January morning, I woke up and realized I could see my breath. Not good. I called the heat-ing people and looked to see how much I had set aside for a repair, which I figured would run me $300-$400 as most did. Not this time. The system, which had been installed 12 years before I bought the house, was done. The only thing between us and heat was a $6,500 purchase of a new system. Eeps.

I recovered, but I learned to look a little deeper at items that I knew would come someday and how I was trying to budget for them, too. Christmas holidays, property tax on our cars, seeing the doctor, vacations/time away – those are the kinds of things we need to think about.

For these items, all you have to do is think about how much you usually spend on each in an average year. Got it? Good, now divide that number by 12, and include that number in the budget you've created above. We'll talk more about how to work your savings in the next chapter, but right now we're just focused on seeing if our budget can balance when we include a bigger dose of reality.

About now, you're going to start to feel a little weird. Few people are taking the steps you're taking right now. This is not the world you live in. In the world you live in, the vibe is different. We're told that going into debt for these "surprises" is normal. We're told that everyone's in the same boat with you, so don't worry about it. Lots of people joke about how they've sunk themselves into debt from everything they did at Christmas. They laugh about it like it's an unavoidable, silly thing. But Christmas is no surprise, and neither is a car repair, or doctor visits. They will happen. And the only silly thing is not planning for them.

>>>

So be different, and maybe you'll help the rest of the world see that there's another option.

So your budget is way more realistic now, but we're not quite done yet…

Goals

Remember way back at the beginning of this book when we talked about financial goals? Those were good times, weren't they? Well, these are better times. This is where we actually get to see them start to happen. Start by picking your first goal or two and put a monthly dollar amount around it, and add it to your budget. So, if it's your goal to start saving for retirement at $1,000 a year, then you'll add $83/month to your budget. If your goal is to give an additional $600 away this year, then you'll add $50/month to your giving budget.

We'll talk more about how to actually handle saving for those goals in the chapter on – you guessed it – savings. For now, congratulations – you have a thorough, well-documented, realistic budget. Well, wait, that word "realistic" is only true if your income still turns out to be greater than your expenses.

Balancing Act

So what does your budget look like now? Where do you stand? There are two reasons to adjust your budget – because you have to, and because you want to. If your budget has more coming out than coming in, you have to adjust it. We're in trouble, here, people, and we need to start bailing water before we go under. So get serious. You can either spend less, or make more. Usually it's easier to spend less and cut back on some things. That's not to say it will be easy, of course. It may mean that you begin to view some things that had been expectations as once-in-a-while treats. It may also mean that you need to reduce some of your goals or wishes.

Your other option is to add some part-time work or a side business to your current job, assuming you're working. This also isn't as easy as it sounds, since it means there will be less time to do the things you want to do if you take on extra work. But this isn't for forever, just until we get out from under. At the very least, we want to make sure our needs are being covered by what's coming in.

Now, let's say your budget balances, but you're not satisfied with your financial goals and you don't have the wiggle room to adjust them. That's the situation you find yourself in when you want to adjust your budget.

Some people have found it helpful to think about their spending/saving decisions over a larger stretch of time rather than just that one expense. For example, a $2 soda might not seem like a lot each day, but when you look at it as about $60/month or $720/year, it might look different to you. Simply cutting out half of those sodas saves you $30/month or $360/year. It adds up! That's money you could put to use in some other way.

The same goes with your financial goals, but it works in the opposite way. It might not seem worth it to save $50/month for retirement. I mean, that's forever from now, right? But when you look at it as $600/year it looks like you're really starting to get somewhere.

>>>

Don't forget to think beyond today's spending decisions to help you save money and meet some of your future goals.

In a similar manner, don't forget the long-term impact of spending extra money on yourself (which feels good for a while) versus giving money to those in need or organizations that support those in need. The cost of that daily soda could do amazing things for a kid overseas who is in need. At this point, I'm betting you know that the impact is bigger on those helped than the impact of the extra money spent on yourself. No pressure here, just making a point for you to consider.

Next Steps

Congratulations on making it this far! You're better off than the 68% of Americans who don't have a budget. Below is a list of next steps so you can stay on track with what needs to be done to put your finances together.

The List

___ Make a list of all the once-in-a-whiles that you know are coming. Figure how much you'll spend on each one this next year, and divide that number by 12. Then, you have a monthly number to include in your budget.

___ Do the same for your top 2-3 financial goals.

___ Put your budget together based on your goals, your once-in-a-whiles and your regular monthly spending.

___ Find at least one other person with whom to share. They can cheer you on or even help! It's well proven that when we share a new discipline with someone else, it's more likely that discipline will stick.

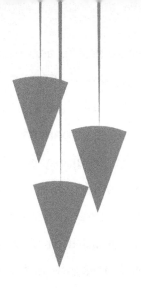

CHAPTER**FIVE**

FREEDOM FOR SALE//DEBT

Never spend your money before you have it.
Thomas Jefferson

The rich rule over the poor, and the
borrower is servant to the lender.
Proverbs 22:7

Shortly after leaving college and getting married, my friend and his wife felt a calling to move their family to Europe and begin working with those less fortunate. They knew they couldn't just go – they had to partner up with an organization who would work with them and help to send them overseas. With a good number of these agencies working in and around Europe, their hopes were high. They were excited to start sharing in the same important work. And while the calling was clear, the timing apparently was not. Agency after agency refused to work with them.

Debt was to blame. Both were recent college grads, and that brought with it combined student loans of almost $90,000. Fundraising was a big part of what they had to do – asking for others to sacrificially give to support the family's expenses. It became obvious to the mission agencies that a majority of the support they would be asking for from others would have to go toward debt. They were told they could not be sent overseas until their debt was more manageable. This meant their strong calling had to be put on hold for several years. This was not the decision they wanted to make. Their debt was calling the shots now.

The typical college graduate leaves with an average of $35,000 in student loans and over $4,000 in credit card debt.[2] If those numbers don't sound intimidating yet, they most likely will the closer you get to your first paycheck after school. If you are fortunate enough to get a job out of school, you'll be offered a salary from your future employer. It might sound like a lot, compared to what you're used to. It might seem like you'll have those debts paid off in no time. But, by the time you've paid your taxes and all the things you need to live on, there's usually not much left. That makes knocking out that debt go from looking easy to downright intimidating – from 20 days, to 20 years. Now that's truly intimidating.

While it's true that there's worse debt than student loans, even "good" debts like an education or a mortgage can start taking over our lives. We need to be careful about how we approach them. Eyes wide open, reading the fine print, looking both ways…you get the picture. Just because we can go into debt for something that might be helpful to us doesn't mean we should. So be ridiculously cautious about going into debt for something that won't last, like a burger. And think really hard about every decision that requires debt, even if it looks "good" and everyone else is doing it.

What does thinking hard about debt look like? Well, your numbers might work with the minimum payments you owe. You might be OK with 15 years of student loan repayment. But the real cost isn't on paper. The real cost of debt is not about those monthly payments or the interest attached to them.

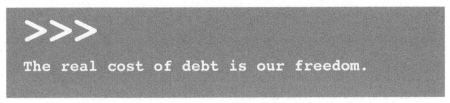

>>>

The real cost of debt is our freedom.

It's not just about things that we can't buy or do. It's also about money we won't have available to give away or to make a difference in the lives of others. That could be a friend going on a mission trip, a stranger in need, or a sudden tragedy. Staying in debt locks us into payments we have to make and takes away choices we could make with our money. It means we have to go to the people we owe first when money comes in before we can go to God with the rest. Staying out of debt allows us to be flexible and generous so we can let God use us where He needs us most.

Being in debt is not a sin, but it is spoken of in the Bible as being unwise (Proverbs 11:15, Matthew 6:24, Proverbs 22:26-27). The Bible encourages us to be cautious debtors if we must borrow money. The changes that occur in our lives (and in us) when we go into debt are deep and far-reaching. Before we borrow money, then, we should be aware of these changes and be sure we know what we could be getting into:

We Become Someone Else

When we borrow, it usually means we want something before we've taken the time and effort to save for it. In other words, we want it now and we don't want to wait. So, when you buy something that you technically don't have the money for, you're actually becoming someone you're not. You're committing identity theft against yourself. This is especially true when you're using debt to buy things that are soon gone (like that four taco combo), broken (your smartphone), stolen (your smartphone, again), or outdated (any technology at all). When what you've bought is gone but you're still paying for it, the fake you skips town and leaves you with the debt. Not a good deal.

>>>

Don't get greedy for what you don't have money for, plain and simple.

What drives us to do these kinds of things? Usually, it's the lie that your possessions define who you are. Who's measuring you by that standard? Probably no one but you and a few others (whose opinions you shouldn't care about, see below). It's a dead end, and it's the worst kind of dead end. Some people live their whole lives thinking that's what it's all about. Then, the closer they get to the end, the more they see it was a sham. In Luke 12:15 Jesus reminds us, "Watch out! Be on your guard against all kinds of greed; a man's life does not consist in the abundance of his possessions".

When we use debt to buy things we can't afford ourselves, we buy into the lie, especially if we think stuff will end up filling some kind of void in our lives. Maybe you have friends who judge you by what you own or buy. Or maybe you think it will help you feel better or be more popular. If this sounds like you, it's time to check yourself, check your friends, or both. You may be jealous of some people you see, whether friends or celebrities, but real life is not measured this way. Real life comes from those things that can't be purchased.

When I was about 13, I was invited to Mario's party. I know I'm showing my age a bit when I tell you that this had absolutely nothing to do with a video game – it hadn't even been thought of yet. This Mario was one of the most popular 8th graders at Longfellow Intermediate School, and somehow I ended up getting a chance to go to his birthday party. I remember the week before, as I walked through the halls, looking at all those unfortunate classmates who I knew didn't get an invitation to the party. I felt so sorry for them. Poor non-Mario-party people. It's the day of the party. I'm stoked and couldn't wait to spend time outside school with the cool people (where I was sure I belonged.) Once I got to the very crowded party of about thirty of us, I spent most of my time trying to hang out with Mario (it was his party, after all). He had the same two or three other guys around him the whole party, and I spent most of my time there (and after the party) bummed about the fact that I wasn't in Mario's close circle of friends. Instead of enjoying the party and the invitation I got, I made myself miserable by wanting more. Somehow I ended up feeling worse than the people who hadn't even been invited. Lucky non-Mario-party people.

>>>

Comparing ourselves to others will only produce one of two things in us — pride, or jealousy.

Neither takes us to good places. I didn't really think about it at the time, but I experienced both extremes in that two-week period back in 8th grade, and it hasn't stopped since then. Stacking ourselves up to others starts in school, sports, and friendships. But it keeps going – later on it's salary, possessions, and family. We pretend like there's an imaginary scoreboard of all these things, and we're getting ranked every day against everyone else.

What if…just hang with me, what if we took all the time, money, and effort we spent on trying to keep up with everyone else, and started giving some of it away to those who really need our time, money, and effort?

We Blame Someone Else

It's really popular these days is to find ways to get rid of your debt by acting like it never existed or that you're not responsible for it. Entire companies exist to help you "start over" or "reduce" the amount of money you owe. Most people (even those with good intentions) use these companies to try to wipe away what they owe, and with that, the commitment they had originally made to whom they owed the money. Plain and simple, we are called by God to make our "yes" be our "yes", which means we do what we say. That includes paying back what we said we would.

In the old days, debt was viewed way more seriously. Two stories in the Bible, II Kings 4:1-7 and Matthew 18:21-35, show us that you and/or your family could get enslaved or tortured if you were in debt to someone. Seems cruel, right? It feels that way to us, but I would bet you that people thought really hard about going into debt back then. They had to own up to what they did, or else! So count yourself lucky if you only owe money to a big company somewhere who won't come after you like that. But don't forget who asked for the money in the first place. That would be you.

If you're currently in debt and looking to get out (good for you), remember this: It took some time to get into your debt, and so you need to face the fact that it will, likewise, take some time to get out of it. Don't change who you are or compromise your integrity. Stare it down, get mad at it, resolve never to get here again – and you will find ways to knock it out.

We Trust Someone Else

When my wife, Karina, began her career, she had some student loans from both college and graduate school. She was inspired to live with a small budget so more of her money could go to paying down her loans. Soon, she was out of debt. Then she had a choice to make. Some of her friends were going into more debt by purchasing houses without any down payment, or cars with very large payments. They made commitments that they were not ready to make financially, burdening them with debt that made life very complicated.

Karina, recognizing how good it felt to be out of debt, decided instead to take all the money she had been paying on her debts each month and begin to save it. Instead of following the crowd, she chose to trust that the time to get that car or house would be clear because she'd have a good chunk saved for them first. This kept her out of big debt commitments and keep her in control of her finances.

Instead of trusting God to pace what you can afford or the kind of life you live, we can choose to trust debt to allow us to live the kind of life we feel like we "deserve" to live. Right now, no waiting. Once we do that, however, debt is in control.

Debt can seem normal, deserved, and even needed ("everyone's doing it"). I cannot count the number of people I've met with who are over their heads in debt and who have the same symptoms. They all had people close to them telling them they needed to buy this kind of house in this area of town, or this kind of new SUV, or whatever. We begin to think our family or friends' encouragement alone is what should be the deciding factor in making these kinds of big decisions.

But, we often do all this without consulting God or seeing how the numbers work out. I'm sure their advice is well intentioned, but they don't realize the demands placed on your life with the debt that comes with those decisions. Debt loads us down with financial burdens that keep us from things like financial freedom, generosity, and saving for future needs.

> >>>
>
> We replace God's timing with the opinions of others.

But instead of trusting, blaming, or becoming someone else when it comes to our debt, we have the chance to actually get up and do something about it. Yes, it will take work, discipline, and even a little sacrifice. It's definitely a different way to live. But, the plans listed below compared to the mistakes listed above should help light a fire to get us going.

Get Ahead of Your Debt

So how do we avoid debt? It's hard to do. Opportunities for that "free money" are thrown at you every day through television, the internet, e-mails from credit card companies. Promises of free plane tickets or even cash bonuses for using credit cards are hard to ignore. But don't be fooled – the credit card companies always make that money back and more off of those that use them, so there's no reason for them to slow their roll – whether it's good for you or not.

Walter Cavanagh is the current Guinness World Record holder with 1,497 active credit cards. His feat began with a friendly wager between him and his friend to see who could get more credit cards in a 6-month period. Walter was able to obtain 143, but then he just kept going. At last count, he had $1.7 million among all these different cards that he could use any time he wanted.[3] These companies were not discussing amongst themselves how much debt Walter could handle, they just hoped he would use their cards.

Credit card companies try extremely hard to get you hooked early. How hard? They actually pay colleges lots of money to be able to come onto the campus and "give free stuff away".

The people at the credit card booth at your college or in your town may be very friendly, but they are not your friends, even if they're giving out free Corvettes. Look, it doesn't mean people who work for credit cards are bad people, they work for companies that do what most other companies do – try to make a profit. It does mean, however, that they are not watching out for you when it comes to helping you make decisions about how to live your financial life. They are not looking out for your best interests. That's up to you.

Get Ahead of Your Payments

But let's assume you already have some debt. First, you have to get sick of it.

> **>>>**
>
> **You've got to get mad enough about your debt to be willing to change your spending habits.**

In the medical world, they call this "stopping the bleeding". The idea is that you will stop accumulating more debt as soon as you stop spending more than you make. That might require some adjustment, but it will save you from a lot of heartache down the road. Bonus points - it will also help you become a happier and more generous person.

So, do what you have to do – work a few extra hours, and find creative ways to spend less. When your friends invite you to go out to dinner, eat something at home and then maybe just get a drink or dessert instead of a full meal. Find inexpensive ways to spend time together. A budget shouldn't take you away from your friends, but it won't lie to you about spending more than you make, either. For some other money-saving tips, check out the back of the book.

Once you've stopped the bleeding and are making as much or more than you're spending, it's time for the next step, "healing the wound." Whatever debt you find yourself in, whittle down your expenses to the point that you have some extra money to apply to what you owe. Most of the time you should start with the smallest debt you owe, so you can get one knocked off as soon as possible. Then, once that one is gone, take all the money you were paying on that one each month, and put it toward the next one. This is known as the "snowball" method. Even an extra $50/month over and above the minimum payment makes a huge difference in how long you'll be in debt. Do not be lulled to sleep with minimum payments. Remember that the people who are in business to make money off of you are the ones deciding your "minimum" payment amounts, and therefore are deciding how long you get to keep paying them extra money. We'll call that a healthy example of a "conflict of interest" that you need to avoid. More on that later.

Get Ahead of Your Time
I have met with hundreds of people in their 20's who are beginning to make important financial decisions. I've heard lots of

good stories and lots of bad ones as well. The bad ones I hear about all the time almost always involve the friend (or family member) who talked them into going to a super expensive college, the car salesman who talked them into a new and flashy car or SUV that was way more than they could afford, or the couple who talked them into buying a house before they were ready for all the costs that come with it. These are all people who are not living your life but who want you to live your life a different way. Very few people seem to talk with them about paying off their school loans, saving money first for what they want, or even just basic things like being patient – those stories just don't seem as exciting to them. But you're not them, you're you. This is your life, and this is the money God has entrusted you with.

One really dangerous idea that's getting a lot of people into trouble once they start working comes from looking at how our parents or our friend's parents live – a nice house in a great part of town, two nice cars, nice vacations. We assume that those parents always lived like that and then assume that we should get those things now, too. We feel entitled to them right out high school or college. The problem is, often times it might have taken our parents 10 or 15 years or hard work (that we don't see) to get to where they are now. But all we choose to look at is what our parents have now.

So we borrow and borrow, trying to become someone we're not supposed to be yet.

Once that ride starts, it's really hard to stop, and it's not a fun ride at all.

So, here again, you've got some decisions to make. Get ahead of the "future you" that is trying to dig itself out of a hole of debt. The future you who isn't able to help anyone with basic needs that they have. This is why you want to decide how generous you want to be first. Then decide where you should live, what kind of car you will drive, how often you will eat out and where. We all need a roof over our heads and to have our necessities taken care of. But nowhere is it written that we have to spend all of our money and then some (no matter how much we make) on those things, and then wait a few years before we start giving money away. A few years turn into a few decades because there's always more stuff to spend our money on. We have to think differently if we want to live differently and be in a position where we can change the lives of others.

The List

___ There's a page in the back of the book for you to list out all the debts you've got right now. That would include credit cards that aren't paid off, student loans, car loans, etc. Fill it out so you can see all your debts in one place.

___ Make sure the minimum payments on your debts are reflected on your monthly budget.

___ If you have student loan debt, go online or talk with friends to see if there are ways available to you to lower your student loan interest so that your payments pack a little more punch each month.

___ If you have debt, make sure that paying it off early is one of your financial goals that you're budgeting for.

[2] InCharge Debt Solutions. "Student Loan and Credit Card Debt Statistics From the NFCS", https://www.incharge.org/financial-literacy/data/student-loan-credit-card-debt-statistics-nfcs/ (accessed April 20, 2018)

[3] Money Magazine. "This Man Has 1,497 Credit Card and Near-Perfect Credit Score", http://time.com/money/4166577/guinness-record-credit-card-holder/ (accessed April 5, 2018)

CHAPTER SIX

The wicked borrow and do not repay, but the righteous give generously.

Psalm 37:21

It was just another spring day at college, and my roommate and I were headed for "the Caf" for another feast. Even if you didn't like what they were serving, there was always the cereal buffet. Nothing gets you ready for Econ class like like ten bowls of Fruit Loops, am I right? Just in front of the entrance of the cafeteria, a credit card company had set up shop and was handing out free shirts for those that signed up for a credit card. It was a joyous day for many, as they felt as if they had simultaneously become adults and gotten free shirts as a bonus.

It wasn't until about six months later when most of those who signed up that day began to understand that unlike the shirts, the borrowing money part wasn't free. Their first step into adulthood had been off a cliff. Day after day they got phone calls demanding repayment, threatening to ruin their credit before they had even started their first full time job.

This is tricky territory. Thousands of companies are ready to hand you a credit card with very few questions asked. Credit cards aren't evil, they're just one tool you can use in managing your money. But like lots of tools, they are sharp and will cut you if you're not careful. If you already have one, or are thinking about getting one, let's hang out here a bit and make sure we know what they're all about.

Need vs. Want

While credit cards are one of the most widely used forms of payment, let's take a second to debunk some myths. Okay, actually just one big myth. Almost everyone will tell you as you get past high school, "You need one."

False. Myth debunked. Air, you need. Friendship, you need. What you don't need is to spend money you don't have. You may have people in your ear telling you that you need a credit card in order to "build your credit" so people will loan you money in the future. But there are lots of other ways to show the world that you are responsible with your money, like paying your rent and utilities on time and in full, not spending more than you make and using a bank account and debit card responsibly.

And, of course, the biggest way you can show that you're responsible with your money is that you don't need credit. You decide to live on what you have, give with a generous heart, and save for what you don't have yet but would like to have one day. I'll admit, it's a reasonably radical departure from the rest of the world around you, but it's also a game changer (in a good way) for that same world.

Again, I'm not trying to tell you that credit cards are bad. Credit cards, like money, are neither inherently good nor bad. It's how we choose to use them that turn them into one or the other. If and when you're going to get a credit card, here are some simple rules:

Plan It Out
Get that budget together and make your credit card work inside it.

> **>>>**
>
> **There shouldn't be any spending on your credit card that wasn't planned in your budget.**

I'm not trying to burden you with boring rules about how to live your life, but living by a budget has been shown to actually help people feel much more free and generous than those without one. It puts you in control and keeps you from feeling enslaved to money. If you haven't already, see the chapter on spending for some tips on how to put a budget together.

Pay Attention

When our daughter Emsley was two, Karina and I had to spend a lot more time saying the magic words "Pay attention, Emsley!" Maybe she was running too fast for her little legs, or coloring outside the lines with a Sharpie. Which got us thinking, "why does our two-year old have a Sharpie?"

People who pay with credit cards spend around 20% more at a store when they buy with a card. Why does this happen? One big reason is pretty simple. When you pay with a card, you get the same card back. When you pay with cash, you usually get cash back, but less than what you gave over. In other words, with cash, you see it and feel it. You pay attention.

People who have a budget are more likely to know what they have to spend before they go into the store. So, before you go into that store, figure out how much you have to spend and then stick with it. Make a list of what you're going to buy and stick with it. Don't get sidetracked by that DVD that you tell yourself will change your life or that jumbo pack of Snickers that you tell yourself will make a great lunch.

Pay It Off Every Month

When you don't pay a credit card off in full at the end of the month, the credit card company gets to make even more money off of you. The companies who run credit cards want you to take your time paying them back. Isn't that nice of them?

This is the part about minimum payments we were talking about before. For instance, if you purchased $2,000 worth of stuff on your credit card, you would get a statement at the end of the month only asking you for about $40. The catch is, very little of that $40 is going toward the $2,000 you borrowed – most of it is going to pay the interest that you've accumulated for the last 30 days!

In fact, if all you paid was that $40 minimum payment each month, you'd end up taking more than 11 years to pay it off, and you'd end up paying back over $5,600 (your original $2,000 plus $3,600 in interest!) That's actually not nice of them at all, but it's the price of borrowing money instead of saving for what you want. Hope that stuff you bought was worth it, because it's probably not around anymore by the time you pay it off on their schedule.

It's what you owe them for borrowing their money for longer than a month, and you're obligated to pay it. So pay your card off each month and don't get charged extra. Don't feel bad for the credit card company, they have lots of other ways to make money. Did you know they make money from the stores every time you use your credit card, too? Don't worry, they'll be fine. If you feel like you need a credit card, go to your nearest white board and write, "pay it off every month!" fifty times in a row. People who have credit cards have found the following rule to be helpful:

The first month you can't pay your balance off in full, get rid of the card.

Something's not working right and you should figure out what's wrong before you keep repeating your mistake and getting deeper and deeper into debt.

Another way to dip your toe in the pool with credit cards is to use them only for things that you know you won't overspend on. For instance, lots of people use their credit cards only to buy gas. There's very little risk of overspending on gassing up your car, but it's still something you want to make sure you can pay off in full at the end of the month!

Credit Reports

Let's move from credit cards to something called "credit reports." Not to freak you out or anything, but there are three big companies out there keeping an eye on you. Well, at least when it comes to money. They track your financial moves, making sure that you're trustworthy with your money and especially with other people's money when you borrow it. Now, don't panic. Before you go looking for tracking devices on your car or listening devices on your laptop, know that these companies can also help you out down the road. If you can show yourself as someone who's responsible with other people's money now, you look better to people who want to entrust you with money later.

These companies' main job is to report on you to companies who are about to lend you money. But, they can also report on you (with your permission) to future employers who want to know if you're trustworthy with money. Using money and credit responsibly pays off in lots of different ways. So, that's their main job. Your main job is to keep an eye on your credit by getting a credit report at least once a year. They're free, so no excuses – just go to annualcreditreport.com and follow the instructions. You're looking to make sure everything looks right and that you recognize what's on it.

Credit Scores

If you felt violated when I told you about credit reports, now you're about to feel judged as well. In addition to tracking your financial moves, each credit company also keeps a score (usually in a range from about 300-850) on how good your credit looks. This was invented so computers (and some people) could get a really quick idea of how good your credit is without reading through your whole report.

While these scores continue to gain in popularity, remember that there are still lots of real people out there who are willing to listen to the story behind your credit directly from the source – you. Even though most places you're asking for a loan will have to run your credit score, ultimately it's a person that makes a decision about whether to lend you money or not. If you don't use a lot of credit, or feel like your credit isn't what it should be, don't panic. Instead, find a place (your bank, a local credit union, etc.) where you can sit down with a real person and talk it out. They may be more inclined to approve your loan once they see and hear you.

>>>

You shouldn't let your credit score dictate how you feel about your life.

In fact, you should never let numbers define your life. However, while we're on the subject, you do want to do what you can to keep your credit report clean and your score as high as possible:

Keep It Clean

As we discussed above, you don't need to have a credit card to show you can handle credit. However, you do need to stay pretty vigilant to make sure your report is accurate, and that you recognize what's on it. You'll also want to keep records of payments you've made (like rent and personal loans) so that you can prove to those who need to know that you can handle your money well. Here are five of the top things you can do to make sure your credit report is helping you put your best foot forward when people need to take a look at it:

- Pay what you owe each month
- Pay on time
- Don't max out your credit cards

- Don't apply for multiple new cards
- Keep the ones you have for some time to build history
- Pay on time

You may notice that "pay on time" made it on the list twice. This is not a typo. Use sticky notes, put 18 reminders on your iPhone, pay your roommate to remind you about it, do whatever it takes! Nothing tanks your credit reputation faster than not paying when you said you would. If you're headed for trouble and know you can't make a payment to someone, don't sit by and watch the train wreck. Get on the phone, call the company, and tell them what's going on. You may be surprised at how much they want to work with someone who takes responsibility. Usually they have to hound people who pretend like they don't owe what they've borrowed. Treat them differently, and they'll usually treat you differently by working things out with you.

Why the big deal about trying to keep your credit clean? Well, lots of reasons, but to highlight a few – it can save you lots of money on a house or car down the road, it helps you spot and stop identity theft, and it could even help you get a job you want (although not every employer looks at your credit report, you want every advantage you can get!).

Lending Money

Just like borrowing money, we need to be cautious about lending it. Usually opportunities to lend money come to us through friends or family, which is why we need to be extra careful.

Very few things can wreck a friendship more quickly than a financial loan.

The Bible has lots to say even about a topic as small as this. That's probably because those writing knew about how tricky lending money can be. It doesn't look down upon it (Psalm 112:5, Matthew 5:42), but offers good wisdom when we are faced with the opportunity. Again, we have to "pay attention:"

Don't loan money you can't afford to lose - However small you think the chance might be, the chance does exist that you won't see that money again. Then you'll be forced to choose between making a big deal about it and damaging the relationship, or just letting it go. Of course, if you have to let it go, you can be more cautious about lending to that person again. But the wisest thing to do is to expect the money or item to just be a gift the first time around.

Don't loan money expecting to make money - God repeatedly warned His people against charging interest to people they lent money to (Exodus 22:25, Ezekiel 18:8, Deuteronomy 23:19-20). I know banks lend money at interest, but God wasn't talking to banks, He was talking to His people (us) and the people in our lives to whom we might lend money. If you do lend money, it's usually to help someone out, so no need to complicate it by profiting off of their need. That was likely God's intent behind prohibiting the practice.

The List

___ Go to www.annualcreditreport.com, where you get a free credit report from each of the three big credit companies that track your activity. Because they each have a lot of the same information, just pull down one of the three, then go back every few months and pull down a different one. Check your report for anything that looks unusual or suspicious and follow the advice on the web site to fix it.

___ Make sure you're keeping records of payments you're making that don't involve a credit card (rent payments, utility companies you pay, etc.)

___ If you don't yet have a credit card, and want to get one, make a plan for how you'll use it, and make a commitment to pay it off each month.

___ If you have a credit card, make a plan on how to use it. Make paying it off every month part of your plan. Don't use it if you can't.

CHAPTER SEVEN

THINKING=SAVING//SAVING

The wise store up choice food and oil,

but the fool consumes them.

Proverbs 21:20

I love going to sleep near the ocean. The regular, soothing pattern of the waves can put me to sleep in half a second, sometimes in the middle of a late night conversation! I'm just letting you know that in case we're hanging at the beach sometime. There's something about the predictability of the waves that puts my mind at ease. Wave comes in, wave goes out, over and over. Again and again. Predictable, and gentle. I'm getting sleepy just thinking about it.

Unfortunately, this isn't how life works most of the time.

My wife, Karina, and I had only been married for eight months when we found out we were going to have a baby! We were overwhelmed with joy and gratefulness, but it was an uneven amount of change in a short amount of time. We felt so unprepared. We had each gone from needing to be responsible for ourselves, to being responsible for each other, to both being responsible for an extra person in less than twelve months!

I often have that dream (and I'm not alone, from what I understand) where I'm sitting for a test or exam in school and I realize that I haven't prepared or studied in the slightest! I don't know how to answer the questions at all, and usually I don't even know what class I'm in. No one likes feeling unprepared, and when you're unprepared financially the consequences can be significant. Whatever might come our way in life, saving money is one of the best ways we can try to get prepared. But getting prepared is a little harder than just waking up from a dream - we have to actually put money aside to be ready, and that's what saving is.

Sounds easy, right? The bad news is that saving comes at a cost.

> **>>>**
>
> In order to save for something we know we will want or need later, we have to give up some of what we can have now.

This concept was so important to the author of Proverbs that it's included repeatedly in the book (verses 21:10, 22:3 and 27:12)

– so it's probably worth paying particular attention to. The idea is that when we use up all we have now, we ignore foreseeable trouble in the future and put ourselves in a bad position. It's the difference between being wise and being foolish.

Wanting a Need, not Needing a Want

One of the biggest reasons we find it hard to save is that we have a hard time separating things we really need from things that we just want. I think we all understand that our needs include stuff that keeps us alive – food, shelter, water, clothing, etc. In college I assumed caffeine was part of that official list, but I have since come to find out that I was mistaken. Maybe I'll start a petition.

Our wants and needs can get blurry if, let's say, I've had a rough three months at work or in life. Under those circumstances, a week at the beach that used to be firmly in "want" territory is sure starting to feel like a "need." But it's not just the big purchases, it's the small ones too. For instance, we all need to eat, but where do you draw the line between eating out and eating beans and rice at home? The difference is hundreds of dollars a month.

We all like to talk ourselves into adding "wants" to our "needs" list. I can't tell you the number of times I've spent money on a want, only to have a real need come up in my life just after it's too late to return the "want" I just purchased. I found this to be particularly challenging when trying to return something that I had eaten.

In order to make this saving thing work, we're going to need to think differently about some things in life. We've got to think ahead, think steady, and we most definitely have to think strong.

Think Ahead

Think about what life would be like if you lived only in the now and never had to think about the future. If you had extra money at the end of the day, you'd be tempted to hit the late-night menu and see how many soft tacos you could take down in one sitting. Or maybe you'd get those new sunglasses for the hour of sunshine that was left in the day. Fortunately (or unfortunately, depending on how much you love tacos), we don't live our whole lives in a day. Because we have a lifetime of days, and every day is different, we should think ahead for the needs or wants we will have that will require money. This includes things coming up as soon as the next vacation or trip you want to take, or as far away as not needing to work anymore one day. You'll definitely need some money for that.

It's really hard to save without a goal in mind, so let's fix that. Sit down and think through some things that you know are coming up that will cost you more than you could come up with in a week or two (head back to the Goals section in the intro if you need more inspiration). Figure out how much the thing you're saving for is going to cost you. Then determine when you're going to need the money, and simple division will tell you how much you'll need to save each month to get there. Hopefully you're setting some money aside each month for those goals in your budget. But sometimes you'll have extra money come your way (woo hoo!) – it might be a gift, or a tax refund, or something like that. Saving a chunk of that unexpected money is a great idea. However you get there, when that event or item arrives, you'll feel great knowing you had the discipline to think ahead.

Think Strong

Thinking ahead is important, but we're going to need more than that. There are a few people out there who like waiting and have amazing patience. If you're one of those people, you have per-mission to move to the next section. For the rest of us, waiting is hard. Black Friday used to start on Friday morning, then it was Thursday at midnight. Now it's Thursday morning, next they will back it up to Black Monday, and then they'll just throw in the towel and just call it Black November.

New movies used to mean you'd go on the Friday the mov-ie came out, now they have night before previews, and now sneak-peak exclusive night-before-the-night-before previews. We all want what we want, and we want it now.

The people selling things to us and making movies aren't dumb, and they know we suffer from a lack of patience. This wouldn't be a problem if our wants cost us less than we have in our bank accounts, but they usually cost way more than that.

Our wants tend to grow, and they keep coming at us all the time — they are never satisfied.

This leaves us non-waiters with a choice – either spend more than we can afford so we can get it now (and go into debt), or be strong and wait.

Back in prehistoric times (I call them the 90's), they made TV's that didn't have flat panels. I lie not – "CRT TV's", they called them – you can look them up. They were bulky, took up a ton of space, but they were inexpensive and got the job done. I had one that weighed about the same as a mature elephant, and I loved it.

Soon flat screens and HDTV's hit the market, but they cost almost $2,000 a piece. Just two years after they came out, the prices were more like $600-800. And that's when my beautiful old elephant TV broke. I went to the store looking for another CRT TV since I didn't have $600 to spend on a flat screen TV. The shocked salesperson told me they didn't sell them anymore and, between giggles, told me my only option was a flat screen. They looked at me like I had landed from another planet.

Looking to stay on my budget and refusing to be humiliated into spending more than I needed to, I went to a local superstore and found that they did in fact still sell the old TV's. There was a big one for sale for just under $200. I bought it and brought it home, with the help of a crane. My roommates were disappointed that I had not sprung for the newest and best, but they got over it and we watched it happily ever after. Three years later I gave it to one of my roommates because I found a deal for a large flat screen TV for $150.

Get it? The same TV that was $2,000 was down to $150 in five years. My life feels no worse off for having watched "normal" TV for a few years, and I've got at least $500 more to give away or save because I was okay with the waiting.

> **>>>**
>
> Saving for what you want is always the slower start but the stronger finish.

Great things can happen when we wait a little bit and throw some discipline into the mix. Sometimes there are things that we think we want to have, but thirty days later we decide that our want actually faded. Waiting helps us figure out how badly we want something, and it might even help us find it cheaper somewhere else. Even if waiting just talks you out of half the stuff you were about to buy, that means you've come out way ahead and saved a ton of money. Waiting and being patient helps us stay out of debt, and frees us up to be more generous people.

Think Steady

Planning and patience are great, but when perseverance is added to the mix, things really take off. If I enjoyed giving guilt trips, I would want to talk to the guy who's lost $10 a week for the past 5 years trying to win the lottery. I'd want him to have kept his box of 2,600 losing tickets (give or take a few small wins here and there). I would show up with a box of $2,600 or so and ask him which one he'd rather have at this point.

One in three people in the United States believe that winning the lottery is the only way to financial security. OK, so people do win the lottery. I can't argue that. People also get struck by lightning, however, and I can argue that statistically you are six times more likely to get struck by lightning than to win the average state lottery. And 45 times more likely if we're talking about one of those mega-ball craziness lotteries.

"Thinking steady" saving means you give up on get-rich-quick chances like winning the lottery or striking oil in your backyard. Those things usually end up just taking your money, and in the case of trying to strike oil, they take your landscaping, too. A good rule of thumb is to try to put aside 10% of what you make each week or each month to save for future needs. This includes things like retirement. Do this steadily and over time you will see from the growing balance in your savings account what good discipline can do.

But let's say 10% is too high a place for you to start. No problem, start where you can, but don't give up too quickly. Comb through your spending to see what you can cut back on and devote that amount to savings. Need some incentive? Don't look at what you can save each month. Instead, take that amount and look at what you would be saving each year, or what you would have saved at the end of 5 years. Even $25 a month turns into $300 at the end of the year, and $1,500 at the end of five years! No matter how small, you'll be glad you started. Plus, increasing the amount you're already saving is easier than starting to save. So just get the ball rolling, and later it will be easier to watch it gather speed.

In the chapter on spending, we talked about a few things that we should or can be saving for. Here are some examples to get your brain moving:

Emergency Savings
This should be the first thing you save for, and the first thing to do before you start is to define "emergency". Emergencies are situations that interfere with your basic needs (shelter, food & water, transportation, etc.). Emergencies are not situations that interfere with your social life. They are not trips you want to go on, and they are definitely not late-night hunger or caffeine trips

Yes, even if it's your second consecutive all-nighter or you're tired after work. Emergencies are also not things you can see coming, like those tires that your car is going to need, or those books you'll need to buy next semester.

You're going to want to set a certain amount aside for an emergency or two. How much, you ask? Most of your run-of-the-mill emergencies run $300-$500 (broken major appliance, unexpected car repair, etc.), so get enough in your emergency savings to cover one. Bonus points if you can cover two of those things.

When an emergency happens (and it will), simply do the following. Three steps! You got this:

ONE>>> Use your emergency savings to pay for the issue, so you don't have to run to a credit card and get yourself in trouble.

TWO>>> Pause on other savings and build up your emergency savings back up to its original level.

THREE>>> Continue with your regular "pre-emergency" savings plan.

Other Savings Goals

Emergency savings got its own section because it's that important, and it should come first when it comes to savings. That doesn't mean that we're done with savings, though. Here are some other things that are smart to save for so you don't get caught in the world of credit. Some of them you might already have come up with when you developed your goals:

>>> Christmas & Holidays – If you have certain times of year that you visit family, or like to go a little crazy on holiday gifts, you'll want to set a little aside each month so you can avoid having to pick between debt and enjoying your holidays.

>>> Car maintenance – If you own a car, you'll need to keep it running. Staying ahead of the game and getting your car what it needs before it needs it is a great way to spend less and get more out of your car. Ask your parents or trusted friends how much they spend on keeping their car running throughout a typical year. Make that amount an annual savings goal for yourself.

>>> Down Payments – During or after college, you may be renting an apartment for a while, but eventually you may want to dive into the adventure of owning your own place. You'll want to have some money saved up before jumping in, so you can pay the fees, have a down payment, and therefore don't have to borrow as much.

>>> Trips/Vacations – If you're a planner, you'll want to figure out how much it's going to take to get you on your next trip, whether it's a trip home or overseas. If you're not a planner, but you love to take trips, you're not off the hook. You know you'll get that itch to go on a trip, so save up for it (even if you don't know the destination yet). This will help planners and non-plan-

ners both end up debt-free.

>>> "Advanced" Emergency Fund - $500-$1,000 covers a lot for a first emergency fund, but some people like to make sure they have about three months' worth of living expenses set aside in case they lose their job or primary income. You only need to set aside the equivalent of three months of actual living expenses, not salary. There's a difference between what you make and what you would spend in a month if you were without a job. For example, you would drive less, eat out less, spend less on wants, etc.

Savings goals come in all shapes and sizes, so pick out a few that are first on your list and get serious about them, then watch them happen!

CHAPTER**EIGHT**
MAKING IT HAPPEN//SAVING

"Saving is a means of not presuming upon God.
Hoarding is a means of replacing God."
Randy Alcorn (*Money, Possessions & Eternity*)

My first car was a Chevy Malibu Classic Station Wagon, dark blue. Yes, of course everyone was jealous. I drove it all across town and to and from college every two months or so. Over time, the car started pulling so hard to the right that letting go of the steering wheel would automatically get me to turn off on the next exit, whether there was an exit there or not. I tried to ignore it and hope that maybe hitting a curb just right would fix the problem.

Three months down the road I got hit with a $550 alignment bill and also needed four new tires (another $500 – that's $1,050 total if you're keeping track). The helpful people at the garage explained that I only needed the tires because I had waited so long to get the alignment fixed, which wore the tires down more quickly. Who knew? I should have. I ignored the coming trouble because I didn't want to have to pay money (or start saving) for what I knew would be a necessary repair – I just hoped it would fix itself and the problem would go away.

One of the best moments of my financial life, however, was also car-related. Even after I had paid off the loan on my first car, I kept making my $250/month car payment. But instead of paying it to a bank or the car dealer, I paid it to my savings account. When it came time to get the next car, I had enough money set aside to put down a big down payment and I owned it free and clear in a few months (instead of a few years or decades). I keep making "car payments" to my savings account to get ready to pay for the next car in full. Once I had that money saved up, I was freed up to give that extra money away or save it for another need.

How To Save

So now that you've determined some things to save for, how do you actually save? It's relatively simple, just put money in a savings account instead of the account linked to your debit card. Based on how often and how much you get paid, figure out how much of that you're going to save. Then, and here's the key: move that money over the day after you get paid. Don't wait around to move it over, it will make you think you have more to spend than you actually do. Once it's moved over, your budget will help you live on the rest until you get paid again.

If you prefer to save with the bank in which you have your other accounts, great. But be on the lookout. Lots of banks like to get you in their doors by acting really, really nice. Then, they slowly take the fun (and money) out of your savings account with fee after fee as the months and years go by. Make sure you have a good understanding of how your savings account works before you put your money there.

Lots of people have found success with online savings accounts. Many of these are banks that don't need to pay for a lot of locations or buildings but instead put that money toward giving you a higher savings rate. A simple online search will usually reveal these banks. They will link to your checking/debit account so you can transfer money back and forth when you need to. Just make sure that they also have no fees and that they are federally (FDIC) insured in the unlikely event that something happens to the bank itself.

Buckets of Buckets

When we connect our goals with our savings, we can see how the goals are (or aren't) filling up – we'll call those goals our "buckets". More importantly, we'll see when a bucket is full so we can get going on the next one.

>>>

We want to avoid just having a lump of money and not knowing what it's for.

Naming our savings will help us know when enough is enough so we don't save too much (that's called hoarding) and miss out on other opportunities around us.

So, for instance, let's say that between travel, gifts, and meals I usually spend $500 during the Christmas and holiday season. We'll round that down to $480, and call it $40/month that I need to save throughout the year. Every month, right after I'm paid, I move that $40 over to my savings account and drop it in the Christmas "bucket". When Christmas comes around, I take out what I need from my Christmas bucket move it back over to my main account. My Christmas gift to myself is not overspending and "celebrating" New Year's with Christmas debt on my mind. That's no way to celebrate.

You can create a different savings account for each bucket if you want. You can also put all your savings in the same account and just track each bucket month-by-month to make sure you remember how much is in each. There's an example of this in the back of the book. It's your call. Just find a system that works for you, then work the system.

Retirement

This section is separate because 1.) retirement seems like it's only for old people and will never happen to you, and 2.) you can save for it differently than you can most other things. Even though retirement might be 40 or even 50 years away for you, there's something big here you don't want to miss. Money for retirement will, on average, be worth twice as much if you start saving now than if you start 10 years from now. It's the power of compound interest, people – your 5th grade math book should have a good refresher course. And because you won't need the money for a while, it's usually a good idea to take some reasonable risks with it. This doesn't mean taking a risk on an investment in your roommate's start-up goldfish dating company, and it definitely doesn't mean playing the lottery. I said reasonable risks.

If you were saving for something you needed soon, like a bike or a car, it wouldn't be wise to invest that money in something that can go down in value in a short period of time (like the stock market). Instead, you'd want to keep that money somewhere safe so you can use it when you need it. But because retirement is usually quite a while away, you can handle quite a few large dips for the benefit of the overall increases that come along with them.

Because you want this retirement money to grow faster than the cost of things (otherwise known as inflation), you'll need to do more than leave it in a savings account. Investing in mutual funds (which invest in hundreds of different stocks at a time) are usually a good way to go. If you saved $100 every month and put it in a savings account that earned 1%, 40 years from now you would have a little over $60,000. But, if you put it in some investments that earned you 8% (not a bad target, the stock market has historically returned 11%), you'd have $324,180 in 40 years. That's the reason for saving early and knowing what you're saving for.

So don't miss this opportunity, and one of the easiest ways to do this is to make sure you don't miss it from your paycheck. I don't care if it's $25/month, because it's much easier to gradually increase something later than it is to get something started. So set up your paycheck so that retirement savings are taken out of it right away. You can do this through your employer's retirement plan, or by a retirement company who automatically takes a contribution out of your bank account each time you're paid. It will hurt less when the money is taken out this way, and you'll sleep better knowing your money is already at work for you. You'll be even better off if your employer puts in any kind of dollar match as a benefit to you. That's pretty much free money for your future. Thanks, boss!

A Word About Debt
You may be thinking I really like talking about debt since this book already has another whole chapter about debt. I do like talking about it – specifically about getting rid of it. But just give me a second to preempt the question you may have, "Should I be saving if I already have debt I'm trying to pay off?" As with most answers in life, the answer is yes and no.

Yes, you should still set some money aside for emergencies first. This helps you start to pay off your debt without going further into debt when you run into an emergency. And yes, you should save for needs you know are going to happen in the upcoming year. And finally, yes, unless you're about to get evicted or you're in deep with the mafia, you should be taking advantage of a retirement plan at work that offers any kind of matching toward what you're putting into it.

However – if you're in debt, then no, you should not be saving right now for the beach house you want to own one day. And no, you should not be saving for front court seats for March Madness even if all your besties are going. In fact, you should not be saving right now for anything that might fit on the "want" list. If this seems counter-intuitive to you, go back and reread the beginning of the previous chapter.

You should also find money in your monthly spending that you can move over to paying off the debt. Get the debt knocked out (see the debt chapter for more), and then take the extra money you've been using to pay off debt and put it to work for you knocking out your savings goals or giving to those in need.

The List

As usual, this list is in order, so make sure you do first things first before moving onto the next one.

___ Find a fee-free savings account (if not at your own bank, another local bank or an online search for banks will give you lots of options)

___ Set aside $500-$1,000 into a separate savings account for emergencies.

___ Place your savings for annual expenses (see the previous chapter) into an actual savings account.

___ Google "Roth IRA" and learn about what makes that a great way to save, too.

___ If you're working somewhere with a retirement plan that matches you for savings you contribute, start saving up to the amount that you're matched, at a minimum. If the plan offers a Roth savings option, check that box!

___ Think about other savings goals you may want to tackle at some point. You don't need to make these part of your budget yet, but be aware of them so you know when/if you want to start actually setting money aside.

EPILOGUE

If you made it to this page, then congratulations! Not too many people can say they read a book written by an accountant and lived to tell the tale.

My hope is that this book inspired you to think differently about your money and where it goes. I hope you'll also invite the principles you read about along with you as you walk through life.

This book is not designed just to be read, but to be used. Go back through the lists at the end of most of the chapters and figure out what's next for you in each area. If it feels like too much, don't give up, just slow down. I can't overstate the potential that you have to change the world around you through the decisions you make in these areas.

I've heard lots of people older than me wish that they would have been more generous with their money. I've heard them regret some of the things they bought with their money that have lost their meaning over the years. I've heard them regret some of the risks they've taken with their money to try to make more. One thing I've never heard anyone (old or young) regret was being generous with their money. That's a pattern worth paying attention to as you make decisions about money.

Many thanks to my editing team (you know who you are), and to Karina and Emsley, my cheerleaders in the process. And thanks to you, the reader, for sharing some of your valuable time. I am praying for the journey God has you on as you make your money choice!

APPENDIX

As I've met with people over the years, I've picked up some good advice from them on how to spend a little less so money gets freed up to give away or to save. This is not an exhaustive list, but may it inspire you to find even more ways to free up your money! The list is separated into several different budget categories:

Housing

>>> Hopefully, you got used to living in a confined space with another person in college, because splitting your space can really make a difference in one of your biggest expenses when you get out of school – housing! Whether you're buying or renting, having a roommate can cut your expenses by half or more and, as an added bonus, may provide some good friendship along the way.

>>> If you need furniture, consider Goodwill or secondhand stores, making it yourself, or finding a friend who's good with those kinds of things. Definitely avoid "rent-to-own " places.

With the additional charges and interest there, you could pay more than double for each piece of furniture.

>>> Try to do maintenance or repair work yourself. Be safe, but be courageous. There are lots of resources (YouTube, library books, friends) that will show you how to do the maintenance and repairs. At least look at those and decide before you have to pay someone.

>>> Set your thermostats to 68 or lower in the winter and to 75 or higher in the summer. Each additional degree (warmer in the winter, colder in the summer) costs you another 5% on your energy bill. It adds up, people!

>>> Search online for ways to make your home or apartment more energy efficient. Some utility companies offer free energy audits to recommend inexpensive ways to cut energy costs.

>>> Lower the temperature on your water heater to 120 degrees. You save 3-5% for every 10 degrees you lower the temperature. It doesn't do any good to pay for your water heater to warm water up to a temperature that's too hot for you to use.

Food

>>> Obviously, it's important to be social and make connections at work, but nothing kills your budget (and usually your health) quicker than going out to lunch every day. As an alternative, bring your lunch to work multiple times a week. You may even find others doing the same who are looking for someone like you to join in on a "bring your lunch to work" lunch group.

>>> Be on the lookout for coupons related to things you already buy. Be very careful using coupons for things you don't

normally buy.

>>> Buy in bulk the items you use most often, especially when they are on sale.

>>> Even if they're not the closest to you, consider the use of discount grocery stores, especially for larger shopping trips.

>>> Eat before you go grocery or food shopping, you tend to buy more when you shop hungry.

>>> Make a list of what you need, and just get what's on your list. This helps you avoid impulse buying.

>>> Go to a favorite restaurant and just have an appetizer or dessert instead of an entire meal.

Transportation

>>> Don't believe the hype that you're entitled to a new car because you're done with college and/or have your first job. Cars go down quickly in value, so fight the system by finding a car that's a good value – good cars are out there that have been well taken care of, have lower mileage, and are at a reasonable price. Drive one of these and pay off your car loan quickly (easier to do when the car's not new!), then start saving for the next one! Do this a time or two and soon you'll be able to buy your car without having to get a loan!

>>> Try and see if any of your normal driving can be replaced by biking, walking, or carpooling.

>>> Regularly maintain your vehicle (oil changes, tire rotations, lubrication, etc.) Try to learn how to do these things yourself if you want to save even more.

>>> Keep the car you have for 7-10 years, or until it becomes too expensive to repair. The cheapest car to buy is usually the one you already own.

Gifts

>>> Make or bake gifts for others

>>> Write notes to people instead of giving them something. These are often more treasured by others.

>>> Make agreements with family and friends limiting the amount you spend on gifts, especially during the holiday season.

Debt

>>> If you're paying down credit card debt, call your credit card company and ask them if they will consider lowering your interest rate. They don't want you to transfer your balance to someone else, and will usually help you out. The less you pay in interest, the quicker you pay off your true debt.

Entertainment

>>> Think twice before getting a cable package with all the bells and whistles. No matter how good the sign-up offers are, the only reason they can afford to offer them is from what they're making off of people who are a year from where you are now! Instead, see if you can get by with a digital antenna and AppleTV and a subscription service (like Netflix or Hulu) instead of making the jump into a cable TV bill.

>>> Look for other less expensive alternatives to entertainment. Movies at home and trips to the library help save money. Trips to the public lake, beach or park can compete with trips to places with costly entry fees.

Cell Phone/Internet

>>> Check your cell phone bill every once in a while, to see what you're paying for and if you are being charged any overage fees. If it's needed, shop for a better plan, or even a better carrier if one is available.

>>> Super-fast internet speeds sound amazing, but evaluate your streaming and upload needs to make sure you're not paying too much for your online needs.

Clothing

>>> Make a list of clothes you need in the next year or so and wait to shop for them during the off-season when stores are putting them on sale.

>>> Don't forget to look online for clothing retailers, who might have significantly cheaper prices. Remember to check out their return policies in case something doesn't fit.

Other Savings Tips

>>> For major purchases, save your receipts and/or warranties and owner's manuals in one place. If something breaks, you'll know if it is still under warranty or where to find a place to fix it.

>>> Barter or swap services instead of paying for them. For

example, watch a neighbor's child in exchange for your neighbor watching your children at a different time. You can do the same for dogsitting, housesitting, or other services you usually might pay for.

>>> Shop prices for any major purchase you're going to make. Spending a few minutes comparing between different retailers is usually well worth your while.

>>> Before ordering from an online retailer, do a quick search for internet coupons for that company. Sometimes you may find an online code that can save you a percentage of your purchase.

SOME TIPS ON DEBT:

If you're right out of high school or in college:

>>> If you've decided you want to get a credit card to start building your credit:

>>> Limit using your card to something that limits you – a great example of this is using your credit card only for gas, or utility bills. This keeps you away from impulse purchases and helps you limit what you owe to what you can pay at the end of each month.

>>> Watch out for fees. Credit card companies make enough money off of you using the card – you shouldn't need to settle for one that charges you an annual fee for the right to make them money.

>>> If you decide to go to college, or are already there, and you need to use school loans to get you through college, don't just sit and let them happen to you. One of the biggest mistakes college students make in regard to student loans is a mental one – there seems to be a belief that you can't start paying on your student loans until you get out of school and they become due. False. Summer jobs as well as jobs on or off-campus should be a priority so you can put as big a dent as possible into those things when you have to start paying them back. Just because you're grateful for the opportunity to go to school and get a degree doesn't mean you should pay for that many more years because you didn't get aggressive about it from the get-go. By saving before your loans come due, you can dramatically decrease the number of years they will be due for you!

If you've been working a few years:
>>> If you find, at any point in time, that you're unable to pay the full balance on any credit card you have, stop using it. Cut it up, bury it in the backyard, put it in a block of ice in the freezer, it doesn't matter. Don't bring it back to life until you're sure you can live on the budget you've set up.

>>> Do your research on consolidating your school loans as well as your loan repayment requirements. Depending on the type of loans you have, your income, and other factors, you may be able to reduce your monthly payments, which gets you out of debt more quickly (especially if you use the next tip):

>>> When you're working on getting out of debt, keep the

pressure on. So many people have resigned to the fact they'll always have to have debt payments. It doesn't have to be that way, promise. Whenever you've paid off that first debt (congratulations!), add whatever money you were paying on that first debt to the second debt, so that you're paying that much more toward that next debt, and so on. So, for instance:

>>> Let's say you have two credit cards with balances of $400 and $1,000 that each have minimum payments of $50. You're making all your monthly minimum payments but you've correctly determined that this is a rip-off for you. You move your budget around so that you have an extra $100/month to pay towards that first debt you have. At $150/month you pay that first one down pretty quick, and then you take all that $150 and add it to the second credit card's $50 minimum payment, giving you $200/month of payoff power. Now we're talking. When you run out of debts, start saving that monthly money or find great ways to be generous with it.

>>> If you decide to get a credit card, and you're looking for the best credit card for you (good rewards, low rate, etc.), a quick internet search will usually help you find a reputable web site that's done the research for you. A few tips:

>>> If the card you're looking at has a reward program, make sure you get an understanding of what their "points" are worth. 50,000 points for signing up for a new card sounds great, until you realize all you get for 50,000 points is a gumball or a #2 pencil.

>>> Don't make a lot of debt/credit card moves if you're about

to aim for something bigger, like a car loan or a mortgage – it makes banks jittery when they see a lot of recent credit activity in your history. If you don't need a loan in the next two or three years, you can afford to play around with different cards a bit.

Savings "Buckets"

Buckets	Current	May	June	July	Aug	Sept	Oct	
Emergency Fund	1,000			-150	90	60		1,000
November Vacation	200	40	40	40		30	40	390
Next Car	500	25	25	25			75	650
Christmas	75	25	25	25			25	175
Giving							50	50
	1,775	90	90	(60)	90	90	190	2,265

In this example, our thrifty saver has $1,775 in the bank at the end of April, and has decided to split up their savings into four different buckets. They already have a $1,000 emergency fund, and have added three other savings goals. They are able to save $90/month for those goals.

Here's what happened from there:

- In July, they broke a window at their apartment and had to contribute to the repair. They moved $150 from their savings to their checking account to pay the bill.
- This left their emergency fund $150 short, so they dedicated their $90/month savings to refilling that bucket until it got back to the $1,000 level.
- In October, they received a $100/month raise, adding to one of their existing buckets and also creating a new bucket for future giving that they would want to do.

Who I Owe	What I Owe (Car Loan, Credit Card, etc.)	How Much I Owe	Minimum Payment	Interest Rate	Due Date (each month)

Monthly Budget

Income

	Expected	Actual
Income 1		
Income 2		
Other		

Total Income

	Expected	Actual

Expenses

Giving

Savings

Goal 1		
Goal 2		
Goal 3		

Food

Groceries		
Eating Out		

Housing
Mortgage/Rent
Power/Gas
Phone/Cell
Cable/Internet
Water
Other Utilities

Transportation
Car Payments
Insurance
Gas
Maintenance

Other
_____
_____

Totals

Debt Payments
Payment 1
Payment 2
Payment 3

Clothing

Entertainment

Medical

Pets

Personal Care

Other
_____
_____

Totals

Total Expenses

Income - Expenses

Month:	Giving/Charity	Groceries	Eating Out	Entertainment	Transportation
Day 1					
Day 2					
Day 3					
Day 4					
Day 5					
Day 6					
Day 7					
Day 8					
Day 9					
Day 10					
Day 11					
Day 12					
Day 13					
Day 14					
Day 15					
Day 16					
Day 17					
Day 18					
Day 19					
Day 20					
Day 21					
Day 22					
Day 23					
Day 24					
Day 25					
Day 26					
Day 27					
Day 28					
Day 29					
Day 30					
Day 31					
Totals					

	Housing	Personal Care	Gifts	Clothing	Medical	Miscellaneous
1						
2						
3						
4						
5						
6						
7						
8						
9						
10						
11						
12						
13						
14						
15						
16						
17						
18						
19						
20						
21						
22						
23						
24						
25						
26						
27						
28						
29						
30						
31						

Made in the USA
Columbia, SC
21 May 2021

38336845R00065